PAWS TO REMEMBER

A Journal Through Grief, Support, and Recovery.

Teresa A. Billingsley

Paws to Remember

All rights reserved. This book or any portion thereof may not be reproduced or used in any manner whatsoever without the express written permission of the publisher except for the use of brief quotations in a book review.

First Printing, 2021

penofvirtue@gmail.com
penofvirtue.blogspot.com

For Mary Ann,

You couldn't voice it, so I did.

Thank you for gently prodding,

for the "you ought to,"

And all the "you should's."

I tip my hat as you play your last hand.

She sat, dimpled in a well-worn recliner, looking at the small glass bottle next to her. Its contents promised relief from decades of anxieties, displaced anger, and deflected bitterness.

It frightened her to think about the other side: What life would look like, what she would feel like if only she could 'let go' and move on? She didn't like to think about or allow herself to reminisce; mostly she just never spoke about it.

She looked again at the tiny bottle willing the fortitude to pick it up, break its seal and drink the contents; to not feel, carry, or see deadness any longer. She mused how she lived life, saddled, knap-sacking regrets that followed her, consumed her thoughts and even her dreams. Regrets she'd never speak of, and yet with laser precision, shaped each decision and unspoken conversation.

She shuffled a bit, the recliner squeaked, and the dimple became more of a folded crease. Reaching forward, she picked up the glass promise, the elixir to absolve, offer peace, and the elusive freedom which she craved for so long.

"I'll just hold on to this for a bit," she said, sitting the bottle back down.

Table of Contents

Acknowledgements	1
Prologue	3
Seasons of Gray	5
Griefs Computation	10
Too Soon	11
Everywhere	12
Just Once, Today	13
What I Liked	14
Ever After Carlie	15
Ache	17
Carlie-isms	18
The Blindness of Grief Etiquette	19
Carlie's Dossier	20
I Will Not (I)	22
I Will Not (II)	23
Release	24
The Casket	25
Winter	26
Still	27
Pet Grief	28
The Other Side	29
Fragrance of Hope	30
The First Day	31
Robbed	33
The Landscape of Your Absence	35
Paws to Remember	36
Pining.	40
Saturdays	41
Of My Heart	45
Carlie Dearest (I)	47
The Return	48
And Then You Were Gone	49
Wholeness	52
What It Means	53
If	55
Revolving Door of Grief	56
Since That Day	58

Between	59
Road Trippin' to the Shelter	60
Interruption to Grief	63
Almost Adopted	64
I Won't Forget	65
Embracing Truth	70
Never Friends	82
The Bells	84
To	86
The Kindness of Others	88
Inseparable	93
In 15 Years	95
The Bridge	96
People Try to Hug You	97
The Third of May	98
To Art (I)	102
To Art (II)	103
To Art (III)	104
Writing My Art	105
Tears	106
The Spectacles	107
Of My Heart	109
The Problem with Dentists	111
Coal Colored Sunset	121
Eight Months	123
Lily	124
Still Grieving	125
Nine Months	127
How Is It?	128
Recollections of You	130
Full Circle	133
The New Guy in Town	136
Broken Partition	138
Carlie Dearest (II)	140
Epilogue	144
Resources	152

Acknowledgements

Anyone who has ever written a book knows it is a collaborative effort. To that end, this project is no less the gift that it is without the help and artistry of talented people.

To my loving family (Taylor & Philip, Zac & Becca, & Hannah) who listened while I talked about my canine companion in the early days of her passing. For every card sent, prayer that was prayed, and hug given, I appreciate the unselfish acts of kindness you offered during the first few months.

To my wonderful husband Jeff, who quietly observed my pain while offering his shoulder, a box of tissues, and relentless support - giving of time and space during my state of bereavement. You are true blessing.

To Jesse Owen who inspired me to think outside the box and unselfishly gave of his time, energy and talent in assembling this work. Thank you for allowing me to share my heart during our edit sessions. Your creativity and honest feedback were so helpful. Bless you and the work you do in Michigan.

To Denee Richardson Varnum, encourager, prayer partner and "lover-of-all-things-Marco,"–thank you for every text of encouragement, whispered prayer, and devoted canine friendship during this season of life.

To Angel Craig who coached me through different social media, camera apps, and blogging tips, your kindness and fruit speaks for itself.

To Amy Crossen, who took my concept of a book cover and created the look and feel I wanted. *Paws to Remember* wouldn't have come together without your artistry. Thank you for all your help with editing and feedback. May you be r i c h l y blessed in your creative endeavors.

To every reader who receives a copy of this book, purchased or gifted, thank you for beginning your journey into learning how one person (namely me,) healed from the weight of grief. May you find strength again, your own "coming to terms" with grief and loss.

Through *Paws to Remember*, I offer the power of hope.

Prologue

This book was written as I worked through the grief of losing my first pet. I had no idea what I would encounter (emotionally) in the many weeks and months to follow, I'd carelessly thought, as with everything else in my life, that I'd "file that chapter" and move on as I always had. But grief, specifically death, permanently alters the landscape of life: things will never be like they used to be.

Walking through the next year in the absence of my beloved sidekick, I became acutely aware of the unusual manifestations of grief, particularly, grieving over a death. Yes, I had lost a pet. Yes, my heart hurt. But why so deeply? And why now? The answers came as I poured myself into writing poetry and essays, and reading about sorrow, grief, and recovery. A few resources provided helpful tools—techniques to bring relief —while other suggestions seemed unscientific, anecdotal, and brought me simply closer, more soulfully connected, to my own pain.

So, you may ask, "What will I find within these pages to help with my own pain?" I'm not entirely certain. However, my intention to help others was one born of authentic transparency; as I traveled the road to my own grief recovery,

I found that writing essays and poems brought clarity, context, and allowed a greater understanding of my own grieving process.

Between these lines of poetic resolve and lyrical essay, I have painstakingly sought wisdom, counsel, direction, solace, courage and strength, though not all in that order.

I wish I could say that grief is a straight path, but it's more like weaving tapestry, the ins and outs—the sorrow-filled ups and downs of every day in the absence of familiarity.

As painful as grieving a loss often is, take solace in the wisdom I've discovered: it's a transition period.
Grief isn't designed for long term cohabitation. It's a time to mourn, to remember, and . . . to celebrate.

Seasons of Gray

She dribbles when she walks. Sometimes you can't see the dribbles until she's gone by. The spots tell a story like Hansel and Gretel, the trail of where she's been. I watch her. Carefully, closely, observing her gait. I wonder what others think. Do they see the pee?

She walks like it hurts. Hips shuffle. Unequally yoked pelvis rocks side to side, carrying an old body. Worn cartilage. Bone on bone. Barely able to get into the car. Scary thought.

She dribbles when she walks. Not every day. Just some days. Sometimes every day. Sometimes she drools. I see it on her face. It drips down onto the floor. Next to the invisible pee. Strength and youth the outflow of a life that once inspired conversation. Her hair, gray. A giveaway. Extra hair protruding from small bumps. Small bumps of facial skin. Multiple tiny projectile hairs jutting out. A lost set of tweezers.

She walks by. A faint smell of urine follows. To care for her is endless. Life is seasonal. Temporary. Herein lies a truth of aging. The ebb and tide of life. Of living unselfishly, of caring, helping, hoping. Of building, restoring and being restored; these years precede the giving of our own life. We age. We fade. Our lives rest in caring, loving hands.

For all its mystery, its darkness, for the delusional misunderstandings of age, the aged, and aging, a life well-loved enters the ever-after shrouded in acts of mercy, acts of kindness. Of support, justice, and grace.

She dribbles when she walks.

And sometimes I can't see the dribbles until after she walks by.

The above essay, *Seasons of Gray,* was written as a tribute to my selflessly devoted black lab mix, I affectionately named Carlie. Carlie had been my constant companion since I adopted her as a young rescue pup, in 2005. After she came into my life, I realized how much I had forgotten, how much care it took to train and housebreak a puppy, to teach it rules. It was very much like having another child.

Gradually, through time and consistency, Carlie became a wonderful running mate, and an effective deterrent to strangers. She often ran with me during training runs, up to five miles at a stretch. Running together became our ritual, something we both looked forward to every morning.

But over the years we both aged, and Carlie began to have hip and joint troubles, and could no longer run long distances. This saddened me. Though she could walk around the trails with me, it was not the same. I knew her body was breaking down.

One day while caring for her dry, cracked paw pads I considered her age. Carlie was 13 years old, 91 in dog years, they say. Those around me recognized her age more readily, but I lived in self-denial, with a can of Lysol and scores of clean shop towels nearby.

Caring for an aging dog, I found, is much like caring for an aging parent. The cloudy film in Carlie's eyes when she looked at me, willing a treat from my hand, reminded me of the way an elderly parent looks at their caring child—willing conversation.

My own children no longer have living grandparents, and I'd never had the honor or privilege of caring for my own parents. Still, as difficult as it was to watch her suffer, to watch her body break down, to clean up dribbles of urine which leaked from her unknowingly, to carry her to the vet when her legs gave out, and to soothe her during thunderous rainstorms, I considered it an honor to have been able to care for my aging dog, who once trained alongside me—chasing squirrels every chance she got.

My Girl
Carlie ~

Grief's Computation (for Car-car)
11/3/18

1/24/05

7 weeks
13 years
10 months

divided by/

7 days.
170 hours.
10,200 minutes.
612,000 seconds.

11/3/18 6:45pm

RIP Car-car

Too Soon
11/5/18

Until I can let go
I will lay on your bed,
    — sob
Let tears roll down my face
Your scent in my nose
tying me down
cradling my heart
in memories
I see you everywhere —
in the yard, the couch,
your bed
fluffed and waiting
My empty car,
invisible passenger,
green smoothie unlapped
brown fuzzy blanket
washed,
still holds your fur,
my tears

Everywhere
11/6/18

Everywhere I look I see her
She's looking out over her bed
at me,
waiting. I get up
stroke her face, lean in
plant a kiss on her head;
the fragrance of recent grooming
dances
in my nostrils

From the toilet
I watched, down
the hallway
her bed visible;
she watched me
A thing we shared

Everywhere I look I see her
Guarded donuts,
gum in the glovebox
covered coffee cup
uneaten box of treats

From my bed
I glance, downward
Her empty pallet,
a collection
pilled fur and lint
looking up at me

Just Once, Today
11/7/18

I only cried once
today when I saw
you
a ghost image
walking toward me
pushing open the door
our usual meeting place

I sat and watched you
look up at me
tail slightly wagging,
door opened
ears tuned upward
— me peeing

I flushed,
you startled
looking away,
the same way
you left
my life

The sound of nails
clicking,
typing letters beyond this life
a world unknown,
Morse code to my soul

I only cried once
Today

What I Liked
11/8/18

I used to like it when you would leave just a few
hours — a sweet reprieve

Enjoying my time, computer, and pen, dog at my side
— edit, hit "send"

I used to enjoy a quiet empty nest stolen hours
sublime — I wrote my best

Lyrical prose, essays unseen, self-scripted memoirs
written from dream

I used to enjoy time all alone copping old school, I'd
shut off my phone

but the quiet — is loud, the house — too big I think to
    myself, who did I kid?

Ever After, Carlie
11/10/18

I have to see her every day
— her picture
remember our walks;
concrete evidence
jarring present reality,
backward

It thunders Nails tap the
floor scurrying mice
hiding;
pancaked snout wedged
beneath, between, shaking

Peeled banana
chunks, crisscrossed
peanut butter capped,
short-haired aardvark
sleuthing tile

Twisted rope lies
unwashed,
fallen soldier — like her,
nestled beside
a blue ball

Her cotton pillowed bed
missing
four paws, a long snout,
a collar that jingled
when she tried to stand

I see her every day
my mind reaches
back,
a place we traveled together;
moments of time
encapsulated,
I smile

Ache
11/11/18

for Stacie

Sometimes we travail —
open our hearts
let out anguish,
hurt. Painful memories
churning
roiling —
a cauldron of insecurity
We empty ourselves
slowly tipping,
releasing refuse
Agony, betrayal.
Broken heart
fetal fold,
      — aquatic map of pain

Carlie-isms
11/13/18

The tapping of a spoon a
plastic lid echoes —
the open jar beckoning,
a graying beggar

In the car I see her
looking out
the traffic
the people
busyness
life

She looks down an
empty cup
Smoothie outlines
her snout
content

Nails click on
wood flooring,
traces of smoothie
still evident

A circle of fur
spins slowly
drops softly
My face awaits
its usual tongue-lap

The Blindness of Etiquette Grief
11/16/18

Insensitive Person: Heard your animal died. Sorry. Yeah, I had an animal too and it died. Actually, I've had many. The last one, I had for 5 years and . . . blah blah blah.

Grieving Person: Oh, ahh. *Throat clears. Blank stare.*

Insensitive Person: You know my animal, yeah well, she was really sick and had this disease that caused her to . . . and then she would get up on the table . . . and I had to take her to the vet . . .

Grieving Person: *Standing now, listening nervously, trying to end the convo and walk away.* Hey, good seein' you.

Insensitive Person: Did your animal have any of those problems? How did it die? You know you can always get another one. I did.

Grieving Person: *Head shaking slightly, self composing, walking off.*

Carlie's Dossier
11/30/18

- Getting up, I step over my sleeping dog — her empty pillow bed; the invisible pet that she now is.

- The doorbell sounds like barking chimes until it doesn't.

- Peanut butter bread laid open, teasing, a canine drools for the toast to clear.

- She appeared to bark, almost smile, opening wide her mouth; a few agonal breaths 'twas all.

- The clock never ticked as loudly, as when the dog needed her nails trimmed.

- An ounce of peroxide. A foamy mouth. Half-digested Christmas candy pooled in bile.
- The squeaker toy never made it past the holiday paper; its plastic voice silenced by canine extraction.

- The black lab bolted to the beckoning call of a slurped smoothie.

- A red box of dog bones — milk carton reminder of the missing.

I Will Not (I)
11/13/18

Greet you kindly as if you know me,
unknown person at the door
knocking,
earnest eyes requesting
service,
random paper trail
left. Little card with letters
behind a name
announcing a title;
let the red-carpet roll

I Will Not (II)
11/13/18

Open the door to you
a stranger
outside, with tiny paper card
credentials,
trifling letters, a titled life
underscoring superficiality,
sometimes
an introduction — a door opened
meant for someone else,
without letters
behind their name

And what then
before the casket comes
and life lowers downward,
the tidy letters,
sympathetic sounding notes
announcing your arrival —
What then
will they mean?

Release
11/19/18

I released you to the wind into moments of time
— a history of guarded laughter, buried secrets,
unspoken events hidden on lock down. Fear's
clutch overpowers your heart. POWs rally:
family tragedy, death, loss; stolen innocence

I released you to the wind
       — tried to hold on, place your uncertainty
I reached, you moved farther away — into the air, next to
whispered cries, invisible traumas; raw pain oozing crimson
— buried wounds of yesteryear

I released you to the wind
to find yourself — what you think you need
What it is you need to do, to stay safe
from people like me, who probe deep
uncovering truths, confronting demons
you run from

I released you to the wind — a forward motion
a duckling learning to swim,
you will find your way
without any help — just the way
you've always wanted

The Casket
11/27/18

It sat in an empty room, waiting for onlookers
   grief torn, hollowed eyed expressions
   silhouette each tic,
the moments between fog and clarity
where, reaching up through the sky, clouds
     willingly part
through which you see the answer. The right
     word, a thought,
the well-spoken couplet to soothe; a mist clouds
     your sight,
the promise of elocutionary salve to transform —
but then
a literary dagger
A blade slicing, thin sheets of ham fall
in folds, perfectly. Transparent blood. Juice drips,
the circular knife —
you try again, to cut the meat so as not too thin
   because you
want to relish its flavor, when what you've made
   tastes exactly, how,
imagination and tongue marry: on the porch of baguette and
     cilantro infused
mayo; honeymooning between crisp sheets
     of romaine lettuce,
and well-wishers struggle with their grief offering,
bow
to a still casket —
     grappling the right word

Winter
11/30/18

In the whisper of winter wind
memories of your face surface
between dirt and leaves
gold and red
somewhere below
you lie there
unable to
offer a
hug
A
word
of kindness
spoken, tender
eyes gleaming with
comfort. A bridge crossed
between hurting hearts whose
lives recognize invisible pain, thread
barren hope stitched to skeletal remains
through a smile whose hand offers more
than any Red Kettle — in the whisper of winter

Still
11/27/18

Miss you,
your short black hair
speckles the bathroom floor;
canine marker
un-swept cemetery

Miss your soft neck
finding the sweet spot,
my face buried
       — folds of flesh

Miss the walks
in the rain
your body hovered closer
to mine

Miss our snacks —
shared banana coins,
peanut butter spoonfuls of goodness;
a three-mile reward

Miss you
at the grocery,
passing your favorites
I stroll the aisle, wondering
how it is — I live
without you

Pet Grief
11/30/18

Miss your gray collared neck
my short short haired friend
Detective, Sleuth, Guard
Sleeping buddy, banana lover
peanut butter snatcher,
tissue shredder,
mint gum stealer

Miss the way your neck
absorbed my sobs,
— red collar, leash,
mounds of gray hair —
tools of consolation

The lake is cold — ducks gone
Lonely reminder
how we met,
how both our lives changed
that day
In the park.

Miss you, Car —
the mishaps, cleanups
throw-ups, and pickups;
the ups and downs of a
dog's life:
the owners
who love them
who also,
grieve for them

The Other Side
11/11/18

On the other side of darkness when
morning comes
I wake,
fully surrendered;
my heart,
my spirit,
my life
safely cradled
in the palm of your hands
Sleep was not stolen
Anxiety hangs —
a convict on faith's gallows;
between starlight and dawn
      — victory's escort
      to the other side of darkness

Fragrance of Hope
11/18/18

I washed your bed today
the one beside mine,
the one beside the couch,
      — and by the recliner

I didn't want
them washed —
your hair, the smell of your coat
embedded in the fabric,
gentle reminders of life
. . . pretending

I washed three beds
      — moved your treat,
uneaten teaser —
the trainer of forgotten days
of youthful play;
 but, not you

Scenic memory,
holographic images
time-looped,
play perfectly;
as I place your bed
back,
next to mine

The First Day
11/8/18

This is the first day. I haven't cried.
Like yesterday, when I cried twice
like the day before,
the one before that,
and the one before that
when I took you to see the doc
The day she watched you as you tried
but collapsed as you walked
Techs rushed in
lifted your body
placing hope on a gurney
The day stretched out
yawning into evening, bringing
unwelcomed answers from untruthful
tests at the mouths of mere medics
What do they really know about you?
I agreed to it all, signed every form,
     nodded my head
Lips moving, utterances. Surround sound of
cacophony
I watch from outside
myself; I'm here but I'm not
Then darkness came,
stars tiptoed out
among the answers and tissues,
offering glimmers of light. I can't see —
a slow cascade, liquid gems,
one landed on your face
I cradled your head between palms,

my hands, once disciplined
now whisper-speak love
My heart spills
offering sobs to the dark night
I lay over you
pull the blanket close
Chairs, pictures, table, lamp,
quiet setting;
a yawn smile —
agonal breath
It happened thrice
then no more

Robbed
12/11/18

Amid the clutter of family needs
Christmas memories unfold
A woeful   c
             a
      s
          c
            a
        d
    e

of tree lights
hallway aglow,
darkness of morning
a blanket huddle
Presents opened
Dad on the couch
cradled coffee
an empty chair
You are there, somewhere
high above, watching
A moment forgotten
       — you are gone
Amidst the gifts, the
wrapping paper
toys and pajamas,
of candy forbidden

When it's over
tissue paper hides
strewn boxes
    — left-over tears
Swept up
Christmas reverie

S
  t
o
   l
e
  n
       by,
    D
     e
      a
    t
     h

The Landscape of Your Absence
12/15/18

I went to the park today. By myself. Six weeks
    have passed
Forty-two days — marking time, reminding me of
    what life used to be
when you were here beside me.

We walked together you and I; heard some
    interesting tales, you did.
I emptied my heart. You listened quietly. Tears poured from my
    soul, I blew my nose
— you licked yours.

You watched me, waited to make sure I was okay
Nudging my hand — wet nose on skin
willing me to move, to take you among the trees
and squirrels where we would walk
side by side

I looked for you today at the park where I first
found you, abandoned
I wept in your absence. Not just in the emptiness
of your nonplacement in my life,
But in gratitude; thankful for being able to love
Even still, more grateful to understand
The beauty of grief and loss

When a loved one dies, we grieve. It's normal. The heart offers up its emotional connection to the memory of a relative, spouse, friend. A ceremony is planned to celebrate the life, a eulogy is given. We remember special moments of time shared with the deceased, while seated in the presence of loving supporters, sometimes in a church, sometimes in a funeral hall.

Then, the ground opens up a cavernous hole to receive said deceased person.

An after party is hosted by well-meaning friends or family members. Coworkers gather around, offering stories, sharing memories of their last conversations, anecdotes and jokes, embracing levity in the wake of death.

Refreshments and hors d'oeuvres are served: vegetable trays with cheese fanned like a deck of cards, olives, some type of salad with fruit in it — and then a parade of treats: simple cookies, moist warm brownies oozing with fudge. A small layered ganache dripping with caramel numbs the grief of even the most bereaved. Tasty confections, designed to put guests in a sugar coma, deflect the painful but heartwarming memories of the dearly departed.

The event is capped reviewing picture albums, watching videos posted, hailing the deceased's meritorious qualities, and extolling virtues surely to be remembered for years after.

Then, one by one in natural course, friends and relatives troll by, exiting, offering thoughtful parting words. Words of strength meant to encourage. Words of hope meant to bring peace. Kind, well-meaning words which eventually become like dust blown from the top of a dresser; they hang in suspended animation, pirouetting in sun beams, taken far away by the gentle breeze of an opened screen.

Some words, however, are forever. Immortal sentiments chiseled in the headstone of a departed loved one, seen by all who pause long enough to read, and remember.

Why is it that we exert so much effort planning for deaths, for funerals, "after life ceremonies," of departed loved ones, but do so little for the beloved little creatures who also bring us joy? Creatures who live in and among us in our daily world, who snap at the chance of grabbing bacon from our plate, licking up crumbs or running after the hot dog that slides from its bun? Fur babies who jump to the recliner or couch and snuggle while we watch TV, or take over the bed, weaving themselves among the covers, burrowing against us with their legs or back?

These animals, our pets, often our closest companions, never ask for more than a full food bowl or an occasional treat. And if they're lucky, if their owner is active, they'll get a walk in the park or play catch with a ball.

Some pets live differently than others, some in big houses, others in apartments or mobile homes, all with distinctive markings and characteristics; even each leash or water bowl may be unique.

To that end, some pets give emotional support. Some are trained to recognize elevated pheromone levels, and some are even trained for EMS or police work. But regardless of where they live, how a pet spends their day, what they're trained to do, or even the creature comforts they enjoy, what brings all pets to an "even field" is the unmistakable bond of love it receives from its owner, or family members. And pet owners, I dare say DOG owners, are known to be fiercely loyal— perhaps the most devoted of pet owners.

So, why is it, after spending so many enjoyable years with our animals, do we, at the end of their lives, spend so little time and effort saying, "goodbye," to them? Why do we not plan for their death like we do our own? Why don't we offer a goodbye ceremony, catered with doggie treats, where other doggie friends and owners come to pay their respects, offering kind condolences, share in the celebration of life, and pause to remember all the joy our pet brought us?

I submit that we *should* take time to remember the love our pet gave us while under our charge—the laughs, the funny personality, or silly tricks. We *should* celebrate their life—giving thanks for the time we were given, to love and care for something who could do no more than beg for your cookie, lick themselves, and then lick you.

One thing is for certain: everyone dies. Even our pets.

So, let's pause to remember their bark, their tail wag and the smell of their paws, while we chew on our toast, watching crumbs fall . . . and forever wait for our beloved canine vacuum.

Pining
12/19/18

Surfing the web — looking
displaced yearning,
hidden ache emerges
reminding me
of loss
of you

Simple memories
everyday moments,
tasks and trips,
the ordinary
now immortalized
encased longing,
of departing
of you

Mutual adoration,
emotional support,
companionship
friendship —
now forever
missing
you

Saturdays
12/22/18

I wake. Not to the sound of my alarm, nor clicking nails circling my wood floor, but the din of distant traffic swelling through the window screen, courting the rising sun. Walking to the kitchen I bypass the front door—retrieving the newspaper; tis something I did only while I waited for her to potty. Once inside, she'd breakfast while I made coffee.

In my office I'd retreat, coffee in hand, journal and computer in the other; I lounged comfortably—sometimes in my pj's, sipping, reading, writing about something or looking up new words. And she was there too. Lounging by the ottoman, often times taking a snooze.

Sometimes when she was younger, she'd just sit by me—at attention. Staring, willing a warm hand to pet her head or nuzzle her snout; the musky smell of spring dew freshly painted on her whiskers. When she got really bored, she'd bore her nose under my hand to get my attention and flip her head up—raising my entire wrist from the keyboard. Her messages were never subtle.

The car was one of her favorite places to be. She loved going for rides, riding to the park, looking out the window, hanging her head out when I rolled the window down. As she grew older, she'd hide behind the couch during thunderstorms, or on holidays when there were fireworks. Soon however, even the privacy behind the couch wasn't enough. She'd scratch at the back-garage door, a sign she wanted to go out to the garage, where I would follow and put her inside my Murano (windows down), her face wedged between the front seat and the door: hiding. There she would stay until the thunder subsided.

Most days I'd meet a group for an early morning run, and she would go with me, wait patiently in the car and afterward, I'd buy her a donut hole. When she was younger, we ran together—just the two of us. But as she aged her desire to run waned; and she was satisfied simply chasing an occasional ball or squirrel.

Saturdays, errand days, easily included a boatload of snacks, since I'd be driving around picking up groceries, stopping off at the cleaners, going to the post office, even washing the car. I had to be careful where I stashed my snacks because she almost ALWAYS found them. My glove compartment became a second lunch box. Planning for my errand day was akin to packing a diaper bag: doggie leash, check. Plastic bags for canine waste, check. Water bowl, check.

Treats for dog, check. Water for dog, check. Wipes for dog, check. Towel for spills, check. Check and double check.

Today as I sipped coffee in my car, running errands, I thought of you, of our ordinary Saturdays when we rode to Publix, and I returned with Milk-Bones—opening the box in the front seat to the sight of your drool. How crazy you'd behave when we'd pull through Dunkin Donuts or the drive through bank teller—that cylindrical shaped tube offered you special T-R-E-A-T-S!

I think about the lazy afternoons when you'd lay at my feet while I watched a movie or, when I was sick, you'd stay in bed, your back molded against my legs, unmoving, until I was up again. How, when I was upset, you'd move a little closer to me, sensing my despair.

It's only been a few Saturdays, seven to be exact, that you've been gone. Forty-nine days. In my heart it feels much, much longer. I still cry. I still wake up around 3 a.m. I still can't look at other dogs without thinking about you.

To love another dog means I would forget you. And I don't want to forget you, or what you gave to me. For fourteen years you showed me unconditional love, you taught me how to love, even when it was inconvenient.

Loving you allowed me to see the full circle of life: baby, toddler, teen, adult, aged, infirmed— then death. You became a precious gift, one that perhaps I didn't fully appreciate—
Until you no longer were.

As I ran my errands today, Saturday, I reminisced with deep gratitude to have been given the privilege to love and care for you.

You will always and forever be, my Carlie Dog.

Of My Heart
12/28/18

Loneliness surrounds me
unwelcomed,
like cold rain,
pelting, stinging,
hurting

Out the window
I gaze at nothingness
the emptiness
of nothing
of missing someone
or something
that was

Your shadow
chased squirrels
Cornered cats
Ran toward strangers
would-be intruders
Tiptoeing the lawn

The kitchen, too large
Bay window too wide,
previously shared —
snacking in covert
between pillows

Loneliness,
Emptiness,
Your nothingness
Fills hours in my day;
time capsule
of my heart

Dear Carlie,

I miss your sweet face. The lick of your tongue. My shotgun companion.

Canine ride-along. You brought me comfort, a constant companionship of many years. My heart realizes only now, just what a comfort you were to me.

How you distracted my pain and loneliness with your cuteness and your energy.

You were sensitive to my emotions—my needs; I needed therapy and you willingly obliged.

Life looks different without you. It feels different. Empty. I have no one to pet.

To stroke, to play with on the floor, to walk with at the park, to talk to in the car or share my banana and peanut butter with. I compare each day, each drive, each trip to the store or beyond, with a day when you were with me. When you were still here.

When you were still alive. When I loved you. Petted your sweet head. And kissed you on the snout.

God's nature surfaced in the spirit of a rescue case when you entered my life. I never knew what unconditional love was until I found you.

Thank you for teaching me *how* to love,

Your forever Canine Mom

12/28/18

The Return
1/4/19

In the dawning of a winter dream
You stare at me
A glass window between us I see your
coat, aged — but you the same
You walk towards me,
I reach out — touch you
My heart spills tiny droplets
On the inside
of my soul
The glass window disappears
I reached for your neck
Softly embracing,
remembering
I murmur adorations of love
How I missed you, us
      — feeling the same from you
You sit, on the bed letting
me pet you
My head turns,
I hear a familiar noise:
toenails tapping
on wood flooring
and my heart
I turn back to you
Again,
      — you are gone.
My heart smiles
You returned
To say "it's okay"
      Move on

. . . And then you were gone
11/10/18, 1/11/19

An early morning hand nudge
Smooth, wet
Telling me it's time
Five thousand plus days
a tiny bladder rouses
carefully lifting
from her cushy bed

A normal morning routine
Treats, breakfast, curcumin
A ride in the car, but first
A hoist up, a warm hand
Seat warmer on

An afternoon. Leisure
Couch reading, reclined,
Cushy floor bed. I look
At you circling. Walking,
Panting, going nowhere,
Somewhere
Where?

Down the hall
A drink from the toilet
Confused slow gait,
A slumping collapse
Your comfy soft bed
Places you close by,
A watchful eagle
Monitors

An errand. Visitation
Alarming text
questioning phone call
Strange behaviors,
body functions
imbalance

Abbreviated outing
Hasty drive home
No welcome greeting
Laying, trunk and neck
Cradled in comfy bed

Uneaten treat nearby

An emission of fluids
An allergic reaction?
A phone call
A car ride
A hopeful outcome

An early evening ER
exam room at dusk
Signed papers. Permission
CPR. DNR. Low pulse, no pulse
IVs, I see the night is drawing near

A phone call, a family group text,
Heightened emotion
An outcome of decisions
weighs
a future of painless

moments
— free of suffering
of discomfort,
for you

An early morning hand nudge.

    An early evening car ride.

        . . . and then you were gone.

Wholeness
1/17/19

Today I cried a bucket of tears. For you. Over you. It was all about you
And you didn't even know it. You've been gone for weeks. Still there are signs
In the garage. The gadgets. Your toys. Things that made your life easier. For you,
For me

Move on, they say. Get over it. Or, my favorite, "it was just for a season." When was
Love reduced to a season? When did the timeframes of nature box our souls?
When as humans, did we succumb to the lie of unhappy reason? Tis a byproduct of a
heart cleft in ashes

Today I cried. Just like the first day you left. But probably a lot harder. Maybe because
I'm hormonal, but probably not. Probably because I understand. When you truly love,
You open yourself to vulnerability. To pleasure, joy, laughter. To wholeness
... And to the pain of separation

Today I cried. And I'm glad I did.

What it Means
1/17/19

Missing you means
Water leaks
Heart hurts
The absence of comfort a fur hug
Quiet companion shared
movie snuggled blanket
emotional reprieve

Solo drives
A window glance
Vacant seat
Full cup of joe

Red leash hangs
Nearby, toys
Shelved
Waiting,
Like me

Missing you
Moments of time
Microseconds
suspended breath,
when loss
eclipses
my heart

In the darkness
I struggle
Pushing
Past,

"Go on"
Like all those
times
I pushed
You

Missing you means
There are days
Like
Today

If
1/26/19

If you were here
I would stroke your head
And tell you how much I love you
How much each day has changed, since
The day you left. Since the day you took
Your last breath, and how in the taking of
your last breath, a part of me died too. A
Part of me went with you, over the rainbow to
That sacred place where love meets death, and
Pain is no more, where memories entomb the
Playful acts of our beloved, the anecdotes, the
Jokes, the silliness of each day, those priceless
Moments, each one cementing — bonding us to
One another, laying a heartfelt foundation so
Strong that even during difficulty, during hard
Times - erosion is minimal, damage so trite,
Love surfaces unwavering at the core. A
Gift of loyalty soothing disappointment,
Embracing what remains from the
Damage of a storm. If you were here
right now, I would stroke your
Head, softly , kiss you and
Remind you how much
you mean to me, how
that you helped me
to become a better
human. To love
when it was
Not easy. To
give when I
could not,
or so I
thought,
If only,
You
We
re

Revolving Door of Grief
1/27/19

In and out of loss
          I'm good
       Then I'm not
        I miss you more
             Than words can say
        My heart tries
    Forms the words
      Water pours
My eyes flood
     Sorrow overwhelms
           I miss you so much
       I cannot speak
          Cannot tell anyone
             The depth of pain
        Who knows loss?
     One who's loved deeply
   I have loved deeply
    When God placed you
      With me
Such comfort,
Support, sometimes I just
           Can't
     I heave-sob
   It's too hard
I disconnect
From all, what is not love,
    what is not support
    compassion,

link myself to you
> to your memory
> the moments between us
>> I miss you.

The gulf
> between
>> My heart — your absence
>>> Too wide
>>> But for the river of tears
>>> And the oar of grace,
>>>> I cross the divide
>>> Meeting your memory
>>>> Embracing the loss

Since That Day
1/27/19

All the kisses I'll never give
I give them now to you,
A solemn tribute of your life
And a love I never knew

Fallen teardrops
Bathed your coat
Lying there
Alone,
On a pillow of eternity —
      — you did not come home

But since that day you left my world
Your world - your only home, All the
kisses I give now, are sent to heaven's
throne.

Between
1/27/19

Between whispered thoughts
Sleep teases
A tired mind,
Longing words
Surface From my
soul,
the minutes
between slumber & wake
When my spirit
Rests
Among the clouds
Where angels drift
Between dreams granted
And souls taken
From the earth below

Whispered prayers
Hang
Like ornaments
Decorating heaven
Each one, a gift
Just like you

Between whispered thoughts
Before sleep takes my hand
Dancing me slowly to a place
Where I no longer see
You, I hold on
Lingering gently
In the stillness of
Your memory

Road Trippin' to the Shelter
2/18/19

I went to the animal shelter today, something I've never done before. Not intentionally. Well, that's not altogether true. I took Carlie there to be spayed fourteen years ago, back when she was young, and so was I.

What drove me down the four-lane highway? The one near the landfill with swirling seagulls spinning over mounds of collected half buried garbage. Why, after three months did I think I needed to see a dog?

But I didn't see just a dog. I saw many—a collection of barking, lonely animals begging for attention and love—peering through braided steel frames, wondering perhaps, if I would pet or hurt them.

And why did I go alone? Why didn't I take a friend with me? Was I experiencing PTSD? Maybe. Maybe the trauma of watching my first and only pet die caused more than just the typical "sadness." Or maybe I'm just working through the stages of grief, and this is all part of the process.

So why is it that I went alone? Why didn't I phone a friend? Worried about being judged in my sadness? About admitting my vulnerability to all of death and grieving? That watching an animal die reminded me of all the unpacked grief still present in my own life? Isn't it better to commiserate over all this with a friend? Why didn't I?

Why didn't I just bury myself in the pleasure of eating ice cream, or a piece of chocolate ganache cake, which always feels less like guilt in the company of a good friend?

I have no answers for my questions, only memories of the shelter and the faces of many dogs—lingering alongside my pint of Ben and Jerry's *Tonight Dough*.

The fact remains that no matter how dark the night or gray the day—no matter how lonely or empty the house, the stars still shine at night— right beside the moon. And each day the sun rises is one more day I have to think about the wonderful ways God uses animals to show us, specifically me, compassion, unselfishness, and love; to give us a chance to live beyond ourselves —to give freely to others like forgotten children, aged adults, or abandoned, neglected animals.

Each day is one more day for me to live out bereavement; the realness of grief which settles upon our heart after a loss, the unsettledness of a new normal, when the usual routine has been abruptly changed. I strive to live in the moment, to work through the ebb and flow of sorrow. And each day is one more day to realize, I do have more strength within than what I actually thought.

Days turned to weeks, then months. Tears fell daily, then weekly, then only once or twice a month. Healing had come. Though at first it seemed strange not to feel sad anymore. Eventually, the gray days were outnumbered by all the days of in-between. Laughter resurfaced hand-in-hand with gratitude, forcing a forgotten smile; and hope returned to a heart that once danced with grief, thoughtfully changing partners after a time of healing.

We all need love and care. For some of us, the need is more prevalent and obvious. For others, like myself, we never really know how much we need companionship and devotion, until it is no longer there.

I went to the shelter today
If only to test my heart and see if it was ready
Maybe
Possibly so
    — I think not

                          And then . . . Emma!

Interruption to Grief
2/20/19 - 3/20/19

Silly little puppy bouncing all around the room
Near my heart, a shadow lurks

Months of yesteryears hang
A cherished Rembrandt,

The invisible silhouette
now pinned to my heart

The red-haired bundle paws a twisted rope
playfully, pulling at it,

Unweaving strings which now hang, frayed.
Like bits of my heart

Silly little puppy — month long foster
Interrupted Grief

Almost Adopted
3/31/19

Sweet little six-month-old with red hair
how'd my heart get pulled
surprisingly, sucked in—
to loving you?

Ginger-colored biting joy
baby teeth near gone,
you'd lick my arm, fingers, thumb —
hoping a nibble, a chew

Jumping flame of energy
you'd run, I'd walk
and watch you
Your red hair,
pale skin
name tattooed
On my heart

Happy little six-month-old
stayed a short while,
long enough for me to hurt —
now that you're gone
. . . Sweet little Emma

I Won't Forget
2/20/19

I won't forget. I won't let time steal your memory or the days we spent together. I won't surrender them to ticking clocks or forgetfulness. I won't box them, shelf them, forget you were part of my life for nearly fourteen years—I won't.

I won't let time siphon your scent from my memory, your funny ways of sneaking my socks, running off with them, shaking them like they were a rag doll. I won't let myself bury the moments, the days and weeks we spent together driving in the car; you riding shotgun, abating potential stalker-strangers, who could've easily wooed you with a Milk-Bone or banana.

I won't forget. The one who walked with me through death and loss after my father died, trotting alongside me during visits to his grave, who happily sniffed around dead leaves and flower petals while I offered words of concession to an ashen grave marker.

I will not—a callous heart, scabbed by years —blocked by the inability to process grief, the part about life where I need to let go. I loved you Carlie, you were my fourth child, the one I never had, but spoke about having. The "change of life" baby who enters the world when parents are middle-aged, with high school and college aged kids; a revolving door of hormonal emotions. Your entrance into our lives came on the heels of our adult kids building their own lives and leaving the nest. You arrived, a rescued pup, with your fearful aversion towards loud noises, and burrowed your sweet little life—right into our hearts. It began with your black furriness, with puppy breath, baby teeth, 5 a.m. trips outside to potty, a new red collar, of vet visits, shots and learning to follow commands. It was evenings of car rides, park walks and play dates with friends who also had dogs.

And then it began. Slowly. Over time. Friends with dogs no longer had dogs. Their dogs had gone to a far-away place, that place "over the rainbow," the bridge over which each beloved pet walks to find eternal wholeness—a comfortable, pain free utopia. I knew of no such place then, quickly dismissing any notion of life without you. But I had become acutely aware of your aging body and the good fortune I'd had with your companionship. The clock had been ticking. And many years later, on a warm November evening, it stopped.

I won't forget you, Carlie Dog. You were my first. I certainly didn't know what I was getting into the day I rescued an eight-week-old pup. And I believe I learned more about life, tolerance, and certainly about dogs, the longer we lived under the same roof. It's kind of what makes families with pets so endearingly special—the times of total craziness, and the loyal devotion towards one another. Even more so in crisis.

This is what you gave me Carlie—devotion, loyalty, but above all, companionship. Your nonjudgmental attitude, even when mine was lacking, showed your true canine heart: when I was late to feed you, forgot to bring you a treat home when I traveled, or overlooked your begging eyes willing a rub from my hand; you showed yourself faithful time and again, coming back to sit at my feet, waiting for the next car ride, or chance to play ball.

I won't forget you, Carlie. I *"paws" to remember* the tender moments of our days together, which made up so much of my life. Thank you for thirteen years, ten months, and 52,000 memories, which continue to color my world like an artful canvas on display. May you know how much you were loved and cared for.

May you forever be found chasing yellow ball, chewing your favorite braided rope, or digging up "kitty treats," on the other side of rainbow bridge.

Embracing Truth

If every day were like today, I would wake up and you would nudge my arm with your wet nose after hearing the alarm buzz. Your black tail drumming the fluffy pillow bed next to mine— a classic sign of your morning enthusiasm.

5,040 days.

Throwing back the bedcovers, I'd reach for my robe and fumble on padded slippers en route to the front door, lapped by your choreographed tap dancing as you raced ahead—your tiny bladder now fully awake. Such was our routine, day in and day out, week after week. Your initial entrance into our home at just 8 weeks old had allowed me to mold your habits. By dog standards, some were tolerable; by people standards, your indifference to strangers continued to befuddle and amuse me. I worked with you on socialization skills which didn't seem to help much. You were a solo pet in a home with older teens and working parents. But you were incredible smart—seriously.

  A snout-swipe jingle from hanging bells at the front door, a trick mastered with the aid of Milk-Bones, signaled it was time to venture outside and chase squirrels, stray cats, chew leaves, or maybe just sniff around. Though most of the time I could tell when you really had to go, on many occasions you didn't need to potty, it was just a ploy to earn a T-R-E-A-T!

You grew quickly in size and personality; you didn't like doorbells, loud noises or strangers —but could be bought with a scoop of peanut butter or chunk of banana. The FedEx, UPS, and mail people feared you—horn honking for signature or pick up. Strangers who walked too closely to our yard, rang the bell, or knocked on the front door, stepped back quickly when seeing you approach the door window.

Critters weren't exempt from the likes of your personality either—nothing was safe: birds, small rodents, squiggly bugs, even snakes—there you'd go, off on a chase, tail a blazin'.

Inside the house was no different, nothing was sacred, everything fair game. Like the 9x13 pan of scalloped potatoes left over from dinner. With paws on the counter you nudged the shiny aluminum pan until it fell, coating the floor with bacon bits and globs of cheesy potatoes. I couldn't —or wouldn't approach you during your scalloppotato fiasco; the low growl let me know I'd come up short—literally—if I reached for the pan.

And your sneakiness didn't stop with just with food. Over the years, countless sticks of chewing gum, sometimes an entire pack, disappeared from unattended purses left on the floor or couch. An open bedroom door meant free access to whatever was inside, be it food, toys, or expensive prescription glasses. And Christmas presents, containing food or candy lying under the tree were victims of your artful unwrapping skills.

Yes, you were a quick learn at tricks, but extremely stubborn complying with the directive "no," especially when it involved coffee and chocolate. Some sins follow after, and you my dear, had many which did just that, followed you -

. . . right over that Rainbow Bridge.

120,960 hours

During lightning storms you'd hide behind the couch trembling, or entered my office looking for safety, a quiet place away from thunder. Typically, it meant you hid in the closet. Well, half hid. Head tucked between my briefcase and a couple of files, the rest of you poked from the bi-fold doors as if stuck. (Kind of like when you'd hunker on floorboard, head and snout lodged between the passenger seat and the doorjamb each time we passed an eighteen-wheeler, or you heard the clap of thunder.) Surprisingly, wedged between files and the brief case in my closet made you feel safe; the dark, cramped quarters produced a sense of calm. Yeah, I can totally relate. At times, I'd wished the closet was big enough for both of us.

7, 257,600 seconds

Sometimes when it was time for your walk, I'd not say a word but simply stroll by the couch with my Mizunos in hand. You'd watch me. The moment I laced them up you'd tailspin a dance, run back and forth, and prance around like a canine who'd just won the doggie lottery!

We both had more energy back then, both loved being outside and running. We'd head off on a three or four-mile jog, with you of course, as lead dog.

13.8 years

As a puppy you scampered about in your tiny red collar, often climbing the baby gate—a lattice guard between kitchen and living room—to roam the house freely. Early in your puppyhood I learned of your unique escape skills after returning home one Sunday afternoon. Entering the kitchen from the garage, I opened the door and called your name softly. "Carlie. . ." You were nowhere to be found. You'd pulled a Houdini!

Searching the entire house, I found you hiding in the master bathroom wedged between the back wall and porcelain toilet base. When I reached for you, a tiny growl echoed from beneath the bowl. I smiled and laughed to no one around while carefully lifting you; I realized then, your need for safety and security. It's something innate in us all.

There were lots of days, weeks, and months of growing and training as we both learned what it meant to share our life: me, adjusting to a new responsibility, and you, adjusting to living with humans whose expectations for obedience seemed more like a game of fun. But, ever the quick learner, and motivated by tasty treats, you sought both to please and entertain.

We'd often play Hide-n-Seek. I'd hide down the hallway around the corner, softly call your name, and you'd come looking. Each and every time you'd act just as surprised to see me, after I'd shout, "You found me!" Then off you'd go down the hallway and I'd chase you while you sought a place to hide. The game was exhausting for me but exhilarating for you!

Tug-of-war seemed to be your all-time favorite game. Taking your huge white bear, you'd start to maul it, flinging it around like a rag doll, a cue for me or anyone else in the family to take it from you. With little resistance, one of us—usually me—would approach you with the white bear still dangling from your mouth. Grasping the midsection of the stuffed animal, or taking the arms, I'd wrestle back and forth trying to pull it away.

Sometimes I was successful, if only briefly. Then, because I was on my knees holding the large white bear, you'd jump up, putting both paws on top of my hands while I held the arms of the bear, and your jaws would clamp directly into its chest, trying to fling or wrestle it from my grasp. It was a test of strength and will, which ended only when I offered a treat.

Your well-being and health were both a blessing and a comfort and allowed us to train together a few times over the years. Running, or rather, training on a leash, became common place, and soon you ran upwards to five miles a day.

Seasons like those are memories I draw from when I think of you: days of fun and precociousness when you were not in pain, when running was easy, when sneaking food from the garbage, a plate from the table, or candy from a purse, were the makings of the Sunday paper comics.

As time went on, we settled into a routine where we met in my office after the morning rush of breakfast, packed lunches, coolers and bottled water. I'd head down the hallway and open the door to my "special room." The one I dedicated to pursuing life and all things that really mattered in the scope of my understanding of humanity. There I'd sit and think, read my devotion, write, meditate, or talk to God.

You never seemed to mind hearing the prayers, my sometimes-inaudible words offered to a Holy Deity whose presence we clearly felt. There was at least one time, when, my head bowed in reverence, you politely pawed my arm: your bladder beckoned—a sign to end my convo with God and pay attention to your needs. It wasn't the only time, but it birthed an awareness— the paying of closer attention to your needs.

So, it began. Slowly. Over the course of time a breaking down occurred within your furriness, without even the smallest hint. But maybe I lived in denial. Your once dark black hair sported flecks of gray, a canine tweed overcoat; the only thing missing was your cap and pipe. And then you didn't want to take long stretches in the park. The same park we once trained. The park we both walked when I was upset and just wanted to vent— to walk it out without human dialog. You shouldered every discussion, every angry sentence, every plea and every prayer. And when the walk was over, we both were a little better off. After a while, "better off" happened while you laid tenderly on your pillow bed, waiting for me to return home.

When once you'd eagerly jump back into the car and seek out the hidden bowl of water I carefully stationed on the floorboard, I now helped you up. You loved to ride and look out the window, except you could no longer sit up for long periods of time. Your tired achy shoulders seemed to enjoy the comfort of the seat warmer, even when it wasn't cold outside.

Our trips to the park eventually stopped, as did your desire to chase feral cats and toying squirrels. In fact, your last day comprised mainly of resting, and going potty. I had no idea you were dying, or even in pain. Your gait, though slow, was sure. You looked at me as always, with kindness. Lying nearby, you softly panted, though the AC was running. The telltale sign came after my return home. You didn't greet me at the front door as usual. Instead, you laid quietly beside an uneaten treat, next to your pillow bed. *Strange.*

When you tried to stand your weakness showed. I thought it was a reaction to flea medication.

But then you vomited, and immediately after, lost control of your bowels and couldn't stand up. I stroked your head. Cleaned up the mess. Cleaned you up, wiping off any trace, any smell of poo or vomit. You were my Carlie Dog: a clean smelling, treat-eating, fun loving bundle of comfort to me.

Off to the clinic I drove with you lying in the back seat on a blanket, not riding shotgun as usual. Surely some medication would perk you up. Surely, they would help you feel better.

Surely.

Unable to walk, you were carried inside by staff members, placed on a gurney, administered an IV and assessed. I sat and waited. Stood up. Walked around. Wondered. *Surely she is fine.*

The waning afternoon sunlight reached through the waiting room windows, her long arms pulled at me, yet I would not, could not.

A phone call to family; dusk fell. Then night.

My mind a sieve, wary of every noise, smell, and four-legged creature who entered and exited the building since my arrival. Since our arrival.

Surely we would be next to leave . . . Surely.

Poetic notions filtered my denial.

The time has come,' the Walrus said, To talk of
    many things:

Of shoes — and ships — and sealing-wax — Of cabbages
    — and kings —
And why the sea is boiling hot — And whether
    pigs have wings.[1]

Indeed, the time had come.

I wasn't prepared that night to release a friendship of more than a decade. To ride home in darkness, in a car with one less passenger, under the sound of sniffles, sobs, and questions. I wasn't prepared to lay awake most of the night. To fall asleep. To wake up. To reach down to the empty pillow bed next to mine . . . to not feel her there.

Neither was I prepared for the sadness which followed. The grief. *Was I grieving? Should I be?* Wasn't that—the process of grieving—to be relegated only for humanity? We grieve only when humans die, right?

The answer to this question is based on my own experience with death and dying.

Grief is the unopened gift left by the beloved. By opening it, you allow your soul to walk through healing; it's a treasure chest of experiences and memories, of smells and laughter, of sorrow, pain, guilt and sometimes remorse.

The grieving process: the questioning, the bargaining, the should haves and could haves, the anger, then finally, acceptance, is what make us human. But it doesn't mean we only grieve when people—young or old—die. It means, when we suffer a loss of any kind, friend, relative or animal, we hurt. We grieve.

It's okay, even quite normal to NOT be okay for a little while. To feel sad or indifferent when someone, or something close to you moves on, leaves, becomes ill, injured or dies. I dare say, the world focuses more on life and wholeness than dealing with hurt and loss; being able to work through loss is a bigger part of our life, than even living life.

Why is that?

When the last shovel of dirt has dusted the coffin, or last scoop of ash is placed inside the urn, those left behind to remember the beloved are tasked with either saddling or processing grief. Sadly, grief isn't much talked about. Working through grief is no different than working through any other physical or emotional impairment. The problem is, we as people don't allow ourselves.

We plan for college, plan for engagement and marriage, we take nine months to prepare for a baby, six weeks off afterward, plan each year for a two-week vacation. We plan a 401K, save for an IRA. We take time. We make time—for life.

But in death and grieving? Not so much.

91 days gone.

What then have I learned in the past 91 days? The time between the last look, last lick, the last dribble of smoothie hanging on the edge of her black nose—what surfaced?

My understanding of mortality deepened and still deepens, each time I confront pain, suffering, and death. My personal interpretation of dealing with grief and sorrow is just that: personal. Every human being identifies with pain, grief, and sorrow in their own way, in their own timing, on their own terms.

For some, grief resolution comes simply, perhaps quickly, as the bereft individual seeks counseling for healing and wholeness. For others it takes many months, maybe even years to process. This process doesn't make one person any more, or any less; it simply shows what we are: human, frail, and in need of wholeness.

Watching the death of a loved one, I've learned that when you love unselfishly, when you support and nurture without regard to oneself, your depth of humanity enlarges. It's what happens when we truly love with our whole being. Yet to balance life, we also endure intense sorrow —the suffering of letting go. In letting go, we mean, to let things "be."

If I only allow myself the opportunity of joy and contentment without permitting my soul to express grief or sorrow, my heart would be at best without compassion, emotionally unable to connect to a side of humanity whose raw brokenness is a painful reminder of my own. I would be emotionally half-developed if I could not, in fact, grieve; to understand sorrow, to just be.

To be, therefore, means, while I'm in a place of brokenness and suffering, I surrender to its teaching, allowing it to minister to me.

The Bard said it simply: *To be*. It means just that: to be in a state of... whatever state or condition you find yourself in.

For me, "to be" meant letting go. It meant confronting the death of a companion of nearly fourteen years. It meant sitting in the seat—to just be, for a while. It meant working through other memories of grief, comparing, contrasting, sometimes reliving unwelcomed events, checking myself, comportment. *Am I okay?*

It meant I needed to "be" right where I landed: the seat of bereavement. And as much as I didn't want to admit it to myself, I needed to be there. To sit there. To breathe the air in that small space. To feel the emptiness, the vacuum within. To not cover it up with busyness and work, pretending it never happened. I needed to "be" in that seat and allow grief to process its work through me. I gave myself time to open up grief, which I found rewarding, and liberating, even in the face of ridicule from those who didn't and still don't understand its process.

Although I grieved deeply, I realized, to be fully alive—to have a rich, meaningful life means loving deeply. And in loving deeply, I've been released from the constraints of fear, judgment, or ridicule.

I have given myself permission to be vulnerable, to grieve. To be. Within this context of love and sorrow, I am.

Sometimes life brings great joy, and sometimes it hands you the gift of grief. The beauty is knowing how to unwrap it.

Thanks for the gift, Car-car.

Never Friends
4/2/19

Grief,
You're not welcome inside my home, my heart —
unexpected arrival, oft hated intruder
Boldly you enter, upon, exit of life
of loss,
of broken expectations
Like a well-worn blanket,
cast aside, at first

Grief,
Your presence lingers at 3 a.m.
My eyes open
Looking into darkness
I stare at nothing
beside me, down on the floor where
her bed used to be —
you perch
over me

Grief,
to know you I must, know myself,
trust, process, let go, work through
"what-ifs," "I-would-haves," anger,
unplanned suddenness,
emptiness, the
nothingness
of you

Grief,
Unwelcomed, uninvited, annoying guest,
my worst arises at your approach
Opposing your hand
to walk the steps
of healing;
process delayed
means life in decay

Come,
Walk.
Be my teacher,
never my friend

The Bells

to Carlie, a most beloved and devoted canine friend. I loved you dearly.

She nudged the bells to beckoned "treat,"
Or go potty once outside

She found my gum or secret stash and often she
would hide

Especially after eating them — the tale of all her foes;
couldn't hide her sinful deeds, while licking at her nose

She nudged the bells while I would write
A boredom act for sure,
She didn't want to waste the day;
      the squirrels were quite a lure

She loved the park and outings, but especially the
      car
Keys would jingle, she would prance
And beat me to the door

She nudged the bells and then would not
A sign for sure to tell, the day had come for us to
      see
You really were not well

~*~

Beyond the Rainbow Bridge there plays
A loving lab, now gone
Her memory is all I have
. . . to muse and ponder on

To
1/25/19 - 4/2/19

To mourn. To hurt. To know loss. The triunity of humanity, of fully becoming, is to understand our relationship with pain and suffering. It means looking within, past the walled emotions and guarded answers, the feigned levity people see, the not centering of ourselves upon truth, the whys of our actions and responses—coring our behavior and coming to grips with our personhood.

To mourn is to be saddened, to place oneself apart where no comfort is, to feel what was normal, is no longer. Life changes the routine and you weren't ready. To mourn means love touched you. It reached deep inside and placed itself, changing you without you realizing.

Day after day it grew, birthing extensions of itself. Little appendages growing, a wide toothed smile, a simple act of caring, an appreciation of nature, a soft furry neck rub.
To hurt is to feel pain, to allow yourself to be vulnerable to something or someone long enough to build trust, to build friendship, long enough to allow tenderness to form within your

heart; the same tenderness that knows love, also knows deep hurt. To hurt means you allowed yourself to open up, exposing yourself: you gave yourself permission. To hurt, is to have a wounded heart, to experience pain from indifference, betrayal or loss. Hurting doesn't make us less whole; on the contrary, we are more human because of it.

To know loss, is to walk lopsided, a once balanced gait—now a wobbled journey. A stag venture unwelcomed - places you in the unknown. You constantly look back comparing then to now, but eventually, grow into self—your own oneness.

You realize, then, in knowing loss, you've discovered the other side of wholeness—the human-ness of life: innate compassion surfaces. Tenderness, empathy—budding byproducts of loss, have rooted themselves in love and kindness. Friendships and relationships are now, perhaps, tenderly regarded as sacred seed: meaningful and lasting.

To mourn. To hurt. To know loss, is the triune stool mankind sits upon each and every day, and the very seat from which humanity can grow.

The Kindness of Others
12/12/18 - 4/2/19

"How you doin' today?" The young cashier with an unmistakable slur asks a customer ahead of me.

"I'm fine." The lady replies as she watches him slowly retrieve groceries from her basket.

"Is this good tea?" He asks.

She nods, "Yes. I put ACV in it." The young cashier stops for a moment, picks up the bottle and reads the content label to the sighing dismay of others waiting in line.

"Whatda'ya put in it?" His slur more pronounced.

"Apple cider vinegar," the lady says with a quizzical look and turns to push her groceries down the moving belt. Seconds later, glass bottles topple over making clanking noises; apples roll, vegetables slide sideways. The belt stops. The young cashier reaches for, and picks up, each item methodically, if not slowly.

"Here, let me help you." The lady looks at him as if assessing and begins straightening the fallen groceries.

I cringe. Not because I have to wait. Not because I'm impatient. Not because of any of that. I cringe thinking about this young man who is working hard trying to make his way in this world; he obviously has some challenges but his determination to be polite and helpful supersedes any constraints others place on him.

Having worked with adults and children with disabilities, people who are labeled handicapped or disabled, I've often seen a drive within children and adults with disabilities— "to do it myself,"—which builds a sense of confidence often overlooked by others. Others, those well-meaning people who "just want to help" by opening a door for the person using metal cupped crutches, not understanding how they've just robbed the individual of another act of independence.

Unless specifically asked by the disabled person, loading or unloading groceries to make the line go faster, pushing a buggy because the bag person looks incapable, or giving unsolicited assistance, robs them of the opportunity to exercise their muscles, to and engage fully with society, as well as feel confident in their own skills.

"Thank you, and s-s-s have a nice day," the young cashier smiles, offering the woman her grocery bag.

"You too." The middle-aged lady with tender eyes nodded politely and turned toward the double-door exit.

My turn. I moved my groceries to the conveyor belt while glancing over to him. I smile with my heart and my face, genuinely glad that I am in this line.

"Have you had a nice day? The young man asks and says, "You have very nice eyes."

"Why, thank you. And yes. My day is going well," I tell him, observing his gait and mannerisms.

He is perhaps in his early twenties with jet black hair, tawny skin and a youthful smile. Anyone who watched him could tell immediately that he enjoyed his job. His left arm showed signs of limited use and the fingers on his hand couldn't entirely close around the bottles of tea he placed in the customer's bag, before me. At the base of his neck was a dimple the size of a small dime.

I watch in curiosity as others behind me grumble with impatience at our cashier. I retrieve my wallet to pay, but much to my chagrin, a small arsenal of change empties through a hole, and onto the floor. I look down to see loose coins flipping everywhere like unstrung fish in the floorboard of a boat.

"I'm so sorry," I say to him, reaching down to pick up my money. "I really should get a new wallet—one without holes, but I just love the way this one fits in my purse," I gushed in embarrassment.

"You're fine," he says, or I think that's what he says. He hands me a few quarters and returns to scanning.

"I'm glad you smile," he said bagging my lettuce. "People say they can't smile unless they have a reason. They just won't. They need a reason." The young man shook his head sadly.

I leaned in to understand what he was saying and nodded. At one time in my own life, I too had said those exact same words.

"I've been in two accidents. The second accident I totaled my car, now I'm partially paralyzed." The young cashier lifted his left hand awkwardly, placing cartons of chocolate almond milk in doubled brown paper bags.

My assumption was correct, he'd had a trachea and had been on life support for a while, a 'medication vacation' as they say, to allow his body to heal and rest. I watched his face, his mouth and lips to both hear and read his replies.

"Every day I have a reason. I s-s-smile now. Everyday. Yesterday I was bored, but then they called me to work." He placed the bags in my metal cart waiting for the receipt to print. He seemed happy that he was called in.

I interrupted, "Then you weren't bored any longer, were you?"

He smiled and chuckled affirmatively.

"Keep smiling, every day." The next customer approaches.

I head toward the exit, glancing back, wondering how people can't see the richness of his life. I think of how blessed I am to have met him.

My heart swelled with optimism at the gift of his service—of kindness to the public; a caring word of hope to others, a feeling of significance, during what is normally a hurried and frantic season.

Thank you, Steve. Merry Christmas.

Inseparable
8/25/19

Dear Carlie,

I dreamt of you again last night.
You were left in a room with the door closed
    ~ Scratching
    ~ Trying to get out
My soul misses you
Your presence in my life

I've prayed, asking God to help me
The heavens are silent
Grief blankets me
Like an unwelcomed friend
I wish he would leave
my home

I wish I could kiss your sweet face
Just one more time
Rub my cheek against yours
Feel your black fur, the shininess
Of your clean coat
The smell of your recent bath fresh in my nostrils
Your grayed paws, cracked pads — a mixture
Of earthiness, grass and some kind of food

I miss the way we'd play together —
    you'd play-bite me
And I'd laugh — we'd play hide and seek
Me in the closet, calling out your name

"Caaarrrlieeeeeeeee" — you'd come looking
Always looking . . . for me
And your t-r-e-a-t

You'd come looking for me, or I'd come looking
      for you
We were inseparable
Me and you

I miss you
My heart can't go on

In 15 Years
9/13/04 - 9/13/19

Back then
Fifteen years ago
When you were alive,
I didn't know how hard it would be to live life
Without you

Without a dad.

Without the advice of seasoned
Wisdom that years of living afforded
And benefited me
More often than not —
at times I didn't even
Appreciate it

And now, fifteen years later
I just long to hear
Words — any words, from you

Fifteen years ago ~
I didn't realize the impact
    ~ of your absence
upon my life

The Bridge
6/28/17

Lord, let me be a bridge which
other people cross
to reach you
Let me humble myself
under the weight of their load
and offer relief at your door

they're scared
        they're hurt
                they're uncertain
                        they cannot trust

Lord, let me be a bridge
a tool in your hands,
wooing a soul
to quiet rest

People Try to Hug You . . .

All I wanted to do was sit there in the moment
Feel every cell in my body
interpret its meaning
push it from me
give birth to expression,
to art,
to the voice I'd been born with but never used
To say it,
Write it,
Sign it
Shape it or mold it,
Melt it or cut it —
To make it beautiful and make it loud
I felt all of that
From one little cell
The very moment
I pushed you away

The Third of May

It came with a thud.

Dropping into my heart was the uneasy feeling . . . the one you get as you pack a diaper bag while thinking of other things and walk out the door forgetting the diapers. I'd been distracted. Life had filled me with duties and callings. Exciting things really. The adopting and un-adopting of new life— a temporary foster who fed my canine longing, consumed my time with unbridled devotion, and left me drained as any young pup would.

Yet in that short instance, in the murky morning reverie between twilight and reality, I knew what it was. Even so, I wasn't saddened; I'd walked through the valley of grief. And like a soldier freshly pinned by his commanding officer for outstanding performance in the line of duty, I'd shed my ceremonial sheath of suffering, abandoned all ties to grief, and donned a flowy bright chemise.
I had arrived.

A new place. A fresh start. Forward motion with my face to the wind, sun at my back, and a hopeful countenance invisibly tattooed to my soul.

Life had returned to a small degree of normalcy, yet the stability I craved left me wary. Situational conditions stirred within. I willed myself not to open the door, to not "go back."

Parlaying grief's process, I roll the dice and played Grief's Game.

Descending the stairway, I give way to tender memories pawing at me like tiny tacks—little blackberries encased in canine paws marking my skin white, then pink; a sweet painful kind of chalk no dog lover gets used to. Here, innocence casts itself in the sweet smell of your puppy breath, eliciting unexpected joy. Pink marks in my flesh from the sharp micro needles continually gnawing at me, go unnoticed, as I bask in the comfort of a tiny fur ball.

I roll again, and win.

I win all those days of bloated puppy bellies. When a string from a shoe kept you busy for just over a minute, and finding little puppy teeth near your food bowl, or closing the baby gate—only to watch you scale it, were surely the comical canine amusements of AFV. A tiny scampering six-pound ball of black fur you were, startling yourself as much as me, the first time you actually barked!

Start here with another roll — a cascade of years flood by. In the recess of my mind, daily memories surface. Like being trapped spelunking in caverns, I feel around-groping for the familiar, to re-balance myself; hoping the exit is just around the corner. I'm lost, displaced. Just like the vacancy where your food bowl still stations itself, waiting to be filled, and emptied (again) by a black canine vacuum.

A hurting soul drained of joy, gradually course corrects as it tenderly steers through pain. Life was the same but really, it wasn't.

Death is a formidable opponent; it came knocking and afterward, I hardly recognized my world. Life had reframed itself. Since then, each time I've squareoff with Death the battle has becomes more personal. There's more at stake. More to lose.

Tabling the dice, I walk away. No more games.

With a brief backward glance, I recognize the ebb and flow of present and past; though the rear view remains fuzzy, it is slowly becoming less distant, almost clear. For the soul who spent more than hundred days crawling through undigested, bittersweet memories of bereavement as it etched truths on the inside of my heart, I had come through the night, swam through the storm, and evaded death—at least physically.

To Art (I)
5/21/19

Dedicated to The Village
I could not write without inspiration.
You inspired, healed, and offered hope during a dark time in my life.

I raise my chalice and greet the day in your presence, thankful you tapped my shoulder with unexpected inspiration. Gifted you are, with your colors—all the feels—and the uncanny way you pull me from my chair, such lure no one has but you; your effect on me to pursue more of what you are, who you are, pushes me—yay even drives me to be better, honing what I have to represent who, or what you are in life.

To Art (II)

I lift my hands in praise for the inspiration you bring; born from a soul longing for more, longing to express the inward man, the vacuum from which the Spirit is born, and reborn, giving birth and hope—in and through man, a manifestation of all expression; its medium clay, music, texture, words, paint. All of it and none of it can describe you correctly. Yet, it's our best effort to produce what you mean to us in our artistry, to tell the world a story, give them a feeling, connect them to a greater meaning. For that is you, Art.

To Art (III)

To every time I wept in your beauty, surrounded by your healing, for all that you've taught me about boldness and forwardness, for the times I've mimicked you—only to crumble it, daring myself to be more than your mirror, for in you I see me; I see the ability of faith, work, and talent take wing, soaring to a deeper understanding of self-discovery. By products of art surface from within a soul hungering for truth and understanding; the expression of this longing, this hunger, produces its own art.

Art is meaning. The soul's truth.

Writing My Art
5/21/19

Writing is a solo art
A lonely art
A quiet art

Writing is an art which breathes
An art which gives
An art that heals

Writing is an art that hurts
An art that exposes
An art that lies

Writing is an art that calms
An art that soothes
An art that brings peace

Writing is a debating art
A curious extension
A soulful expression

Writing is art
A soul tattoo
Immortally inked

Writing is breath
Writing is life
To write,
is to live

Tears
6/4/19

for Elizabeth Smart—I'll weep for you.

Tears fall from heaven
when innocence is robbed
Brokenness from breaking laws,
birthing such macabre

Tears from heaven pool
on the soil of indiscretion
mirroring the minor-ing
and all that's left to guess in

Tears fall beneath her lids
privately she copes,
praying that tomorrow brings
a miracle of hope

Tears from heaven bathe a soul
whose words cannot give voice,
 especially to those entrapped —
to those not given choice

The Spectacles

She saw the spectacles, unwillingly tried them on. Other people wore them. Some wore them perched on their nose as they read, looking studious. Others wore them and as they spoke in conversation or observed surrounding events, glancing above the frames.

The oft-worn necessary detail felt like part of her body, a floating appendage which migrated from nose to head, then back to nose. And sometimes it just dangled from a small chain hung loosely around her neck. Always present—the little weight that it has come to be.

It appears that eventually almost all humans confront the intrusion of wearing, or rather, the necessity of wearing, spectacles.

Spectacles. The foreign object which rests on human nose, sometimes decorative, but oftentimes not, more regularly becomes the costly accoutrement intended to see things more clearly. At the very least, the wearing of spectacles is personal.

The idea of physical contact with an emotionless, mass manufactured object, can be daunting. So many choices, styles—colors. Then, the trauma of "fitting;" the idea of how spectacles look to others, or why it matters. At times, with varying frequency, spectacles—the wearing and choosing of, and fitting of said item, causes great division. Best to leave choices to self and avoid unnecessary tension.

One thing for certain, once you've been handed spectacles, life is hardly the same: your vision is forever altered, permanently changed. What once was foreign, an object appearing on the faces of others, now becomes an unwelcome acquaintance.

Oddly enough and perhaps a little sad, over time, you'll become more familiar with each other. You'll experience new forms and sizes in the wearing of spectacles; each one will be different.

Each one will alter your vision just a little bit more.

It is, after all, how we see life.

Through spectacles.

Spectacles = death, the image of dying, a funeral, the choosing of caskets.

Of My Heart
12/28/18

Loneliness surrounds me
unwelcomed, like cold rain,
pelting, stinging,
hurting

Out the window
I gaze at nothingness
the emptiness
of nothing
of missing someone
or something that was

Your shadow
chased squirrels
Cornered cats
Ran toward strangers
would-be intruders
Tiptoeing the lawn

The kitchen, too large
Bay window too wide,
previously shared -
snacking in covert
between pillows

Loneliness,
Emptiness,
Your nothingness
Fills hours
in my day;
time capsule
of my heart

"No, Thank you. That will never be an option for me," I reply to the assistant scheduling my midyear dental cleaning when she offers fluoride treatments.

"Yes, Ms. Billingsley, you've mentioned that before but—" the assistant hesitates briefly, "here in our office we always let the patient know their options."

I bristled at her answer remembering how long it took me to walk without pain, breathe normally without coughing, and to regain my strength and stamina.

"I was poisoned", I said carefully, "by a medication containing fluoride, and it took me a long time to recover . . ."

"All medications have ingredients of one form or another which can do harm." I interrupted the assistant.

"Exactly my point!" I tell her. "It's why I strive NOT to take antibiotics, or meds with fluoride in them."

My words came out forceful but not unkind. As a patient I felt disrespected; my own health was in jeopardy. I felt like the dentist, or rather his staff, didn't have MY best interests in mind.

~*~

Just eighteen months earlier, over a weekend, I had started feeling run down, and by Sunday evening I was flat on my back-nursing body aches and a temperature. *Maybe I just need to sleep this off. Maybe I'm just run down.*

I got up slowly the next day and took Tylenol to keep my pain tolerable, knowing I had an hour commute to a work meeting. I felt "okay," but definitely not well. I muscled through the work conference as best as I could.

During the drive back to the office I turned my seat warmer on. It was early March in Florida, but I was cold, and my eyes were watery. I also felt tired—zapped of energy. Having no energy was new for me. I was used to pulling late nights; having raised three kids, there was always work to be done, papers to write for college, school projects to help with. Those years were well behind me and my husband now. It seemed strange to feel so worn out.

I pulled into a Dunkin Donuts, got a cup of tea, and nursed it on the drive home, hoping it would warm me, and make me feel better.

Later that afternoon I laid on the couch, bundled in blankets. My symptoms were still the same, except worse. Horrible body aches, severe fatigue and low temp of 100. I fluctuated between sweats and chills, which was a new symptom. I'd never had chills before when I was sick, my body shook uncontrollably at times.

"You're scaring me Teresa," My husband said, looking over from his computer, straining to catch a glimpse of my face. My makeshift cocoon muffled my words—he walked to the couch and sat down next to me.

I moved the blanket from my mouth. "It's kind of scary for me too."

In all my years of working at a busy surgical office I had never encountered an illness I couldn't shake off or just work through, until now.

"I'll call the doctor tomorrow if I'm no better in the morning." I said, slinking down again into my cocoon. *Hopefully this is just a 48-hour virus.*

When morning came, I was worse. My "bark" sounded like some kind of croup, my temp was over 100, and now, severe body aches racked me all over.

"I've been hit by a Mack Truck," I say to the figure behind the foggy shower door as I retrieved a familiar red and white Tylenol bottle from the medicine cabinet and phoned my doctor's office.

"Call the doctor. See if you can get in today," my husband yells between shampoos.

Later that morning I sit in an exam room waiting for the nurse to finish my vitals.

"Well, your temperature is close to normal, Ms. Billingsley." She looked at me almost in suspicion.

"That's because I just took two Tylenol less than an hour ago," I tell her, coughing between words. I look in my purse for a tissue to cover my mouth as she continued.

"Well, if I had a lasso, I could wrap it around Marion County three times, for as many cases of the flu as we've seen this week. I can pretty much guarantee that's what you have."

I stare at her blankly, not saying a word. *What in the world was she talking about?*

The nurse exited finally, and after a few minutes, an ARNP, covering for my doctor, entered.

"Hello Ms. Billingsley, I'm Susan. I hear you're not feeling well." She appeared tall, with short brown hair and a soft voice, wearing a lab coat sporting her name, title, and credentials embroidered on the left lapel.

Her medically trained eyes assessed my profile and demeanor, she readied her stethoscope, then listened to my heart and back. Afterward she looked into my ears, and my throat.

As she stood up, she made her diagnosis:

"Well, I don't see any signs of infection. You're not blowing or coughing green. It's probably a strong case of the flu. We've seen a lot of that this year."

What is wrong with you people? This is NOT normal for me! I know my body—my chest hurts, I have a low-grade fever. I can barely walk —I have no energy. Won't you order an x-ray?

I stared at the Nurse Practitioner the same way I did the triage nurse and shook my head.

"How long have you been feeling this way?" She asked.

"Well," I said, "I could tell something was not right on Saturday morning. I was not feeling well, and it got progressively worse."

"So, it's just been four days," she says, "I recommend staying in bed and taking Tylenol for your body aches and over-the-counter meds to help with your cough. You should start to feel better in a couple days."

As directed, I call out sick, get a doctor's note faxed to my office.

Later that afternoon, I laid on the couch bundled in blankets - plagued by horrible body aches, severe fatigue and a low-grade temp of 100. My symptoms had worsened in severity and intensity. Though my cough was only slight, I didn't have the energy to bring up the congestion brewing in my chest. Without appetite, my only nutrition was hot tea, water and Sprite.

I loathed the thought of standing in the kitchen trying to make something to eat. *Do I have the strength to move a chair to the stove, so I can sit while I heat soup? Forget it.*

My husband tried to comfort, but I didn't want him getting sick either. He slept in our guest room because my cough woke him during the night. Really, I coughed more at night than during the day. M*aybe that's what's making me tired during the day—all this nighttime coughing.*

"How long are you going to wait until you call them again?" My husband's concerned voice sent an alarm signal. "You've been doctoring yourself, and you're no better," he said, pulling up his jeans, tucking in his shirt, securing his belt and then walking over. "I really think you should call again," he said softly, with a side-hug goodbye.

Later that morning at the doctor's office, I zip my jacket all the way up, pinching the skin on my neck as I sit in the waiting room. I'm the only person with a coat on. I haven't coughed much this morning, and I'm not sure if I have a fever. I didn't have the energy to open the cabinet and take a Tylenol, much less my own temperature. I sat with my eyes closed and listened to the buzzing sound in my ears, the kind your head makes when it's clogged or foggy.

"Ms. Billingsley?" A nurse called out. I look up at her, half-wondering if I can stand.

"Uh, yes? I ambled over.

"Let's get your weight and vitals." I look at her, offering a weak smile. I see she's not the same nurse as before, and walk toward the scale with my shoes, coat, belt, and everything else—too weak to struggle with taking them off, and dreading the thought of having to put it all back on. I don't care what the scale says today.

Once in the exam room, the nurse questions my visit. My response is nearly whispered.

"I'm worse than Tuesday. My cough, body pain, and aches . . . Usually, I can shake off a sickness in a couple of days . . ." my voice trailed.

She makes a few notes in my chart, checks my blood pressure and temp, and assures me she'll return. A few minutes later, the nurse practitioner arrives. She asks me the exact same questions as the triage nurse. I want to roll my eyes but didn't. *Seriously?* I repeated my symptoms in the same whispered voice. Then she takes her stethoscope and listens to my back and my chest.

"I'd like to order a chest x-ray?" she looked at me with a mildly quizzical but serious face.

"Do I have to drive anywhere?" I asked. "I'm not really feeling all that well . . ."

"We have an onsite radiology staff and can do it here." Her answer was a welcomed reprieve.

"Okay," I agreed weakly and walked to another waiting room where a medical tech hands me a short hospital gown and tells me to undress.

She notices my shivering, then offers a second one.

I stand in front of a screen with my arms down. Once in place, the tech asked, "Will you please raise your arms and turn to your left?" When I do, the gown falls slightly, exposing my arms, making me feel colder.

Goosebumps form immediately. Silently I pray it won't take much longer. *Can I stand and sleep at the same time?*

"Turn to your right, please." Her command was polite. "Hold your breath."

Back in the exam room I wait for the nurse. Having worked in the medical field, I knew chest x-rays can take a day or so for the results. Unsure of what was next, I lean back in my chair, jacket re-zipped with eyes closed. *I could sleep for a year.*

"Ms. Billingsley?" a voice calls from outside my exam room - the door opens. I struggled to sit up and squint at her, feeling a weight in my chest, and undeniable fatigue.

"Yes?"

"We received your x-ray report already and it appears you have pneumonia in your left lung." The nurse practitioner looked at me a little worried and began a barrage of questions about medications and allergies.

I could hear a voice, but a dazed fog kept me from listening, or truly, even caring. I consented to it all, without any research on the injections I'm given, what I'll be swallowing, or inhaling.

Down the rabbit hole I slid, a dark tunnel where pain fueled tart responses, and the only strength I had left was to cough, which I did often, and most violently. No fighting. No resisting. Just "fix me;" make the pain go away. I just wanted to sleep forever.

My road to recovery from pneumonia was a long one. A road potholed with allergic reactions and side-affects from medications which kept me sidelined for a while.

When I finally became healthy enough to do some research—my **"How did this happen?"** moment—I traced my illness partly to nutritional deficiencies. But mainly, it was a

lack of education —a lack of doing my own homework, of fact checking labels, of researching drug interactions with my own known allergies—which set me back.
Not just once with pneumonia, but twice.

I'm back in the dentist's waiting room again; the receptionist looks up at me and pauses; she's waiting to schedule a follow-up time. Shaken from my reverie and thinking of how blessed I am to have recovered, I answer her.

"The first appointment after lunch please," I say as she hands me a card.

"Of course," she says. Then adds smugly, "One six-month cleaning WITHOUT fluoride treatment!"

Leaving the office, I wondered how many others like her are unaware of the dangers of fluoride, of FQ medications, medical treatments, or prescriptions taken without proper research, and the catastrophic fallout to both immune system, and brain function because of it.

I shake my head while heading to my car, rehearsing once again, a personal mantra to protect my own health.

Coal Colored Sunset
6/20/19

Where did you go? I left you lying. There, on the floor. Your heather speckled snout wedged halfway between ridges of downy bedding. Sleeping. Breathing. Occasional paws waving in the air, synchronized motions with eyes twitching, dreaming—chasing.

>You were dying.
>
>I was clueless.
>
>Just out running errands.

~*~

A sticky, bile-colored substance pooled next to an uneaten Milk-Bone, the Milk-Bone lying next to you on the floor. Your organs shut down. I shut out reality, the truth of what was happening. You laid there. Grossly thickened midsection, irregular chunk of statuesque coal, curled on gray laminate — blended streaks of gray. Carried to the car—a towel-draped canine who'd lost body function, squirming slightly in the backseat.

>I drove to the vet watching the rear-view mirror.

The sun began setting.

~*~

Where did you meander off to? I stroked your head, looked into your eyes. Your telling eyes. Non-responsive, vacant eyes. Eyes that looked away in guilt after sneaking gum from my purse, or snacks from the car, or food from the counter. They always told on you. Like now. Something was terribly wrong.

 My husband texted. The tech drew labs.

 I grabbed a Kleenex.

Eight Months
7/3/19

I cried myself to sleep last night. Again
Not because I was angry
Or because I was mad
I cried because the hole in my life held me
prisoner;
Handcuffed by emptiness the moments of each
    day, each night, are but tiny links
Chaining me
to a memory
of you

Last night it swallowed me. I fell to the bottom
In an abyss of blackness; there I felt for you
For comfort, the familiar softness of kind eyes and
acceptance
The place of safety where words from
conversation could not confuse meaning
I looked for your face
But you were not
You could not
Be there

I cried last night, and again today. I looked at your
    picture
Remembered our times together, the fun we had,
    the rides we took,
The games we played, and the joy we shared.
It's been eight months
since you left

And I still cry

Lily
7/15/19

The sweetness of your face drew me
Like a moth to a flame; your soft brown eyes
    shone
With love and gentleness

I couldn't help myself
I looked for you each day
Hoping

To steal a glimpse when you walked by
Your gold-blond hair with wispy tendrils
Wrapped itself around my heart

It was the first time, I think
I opened my heart to love
Since the day love died

But you allowed me
To be your friend. To show affection
To give and receive love again
Thank you

It was the sweetness of your face
Which drew me,
soft brown eyes and gold-blond hair,
. . . your canine calling card

Still Grieving

I
look for you
the face of every dog I see
walking with their master
search for you, for the familiar
jaunt, the look in your eye —
all knowing sense of "a treat" nearby

I
long for you,
the car ride companionship
Protector-Extraordinaire —
coffee lapping canine;
your sole mission:
servicing my heart

I
Could never forget
All the good you gave
Layered between
Frustrations — a missing sock
Pack of gum, or pan of potatoes saved
Then pushed to the floor — a salivating hunk of
Canine energy going for broke
Could another dog fill the hole
Replace the longing,
assuage the ache?
Could I ever recreate what we had?

I
cry for you
the empty days of dog-less-ness
seep into my life — blanketing
me with your absence
>   Maybe it's your memory that I miss the most
>   The thing that we had
>   14 years together
>   A meaningful symbiotic flow of give and take
>   Much like a marriage

I still grieve, even now
Because I loved you
Because I miss you
Because I miss us

Nine Months
8/12/19

I still miss you when I lie down
at night
snorkeled breathing —
light scratching
the dream of catching
a squirrel
The constant variable
In my crazy world,
You added value to my life
In ways I never realized

To "walk" you meant a nudge,
The wetness of your nose
Against my leg,
Sniffing green hitchhikers,
grass on my shoes
Then off you'd look
The distant sky, calling

We walked together —
You and I
A life of many years
Untold stories
From my lips
To your ears
Canine secrets,
Best friends for life

And I still miss you

How Is It?
8/25/19

After nine months I still dream about you
    — The void of your life permeates mine
The days clip by like race cars, I fill my time with service
to others, to projects, to family
And yet it's still there
No matter how busy
I become
That I can't shake your last days
The way you'd hide behind the couch
 Without a storm brewing
 Hiding from me? the pain?
Impending forecast of death?
Parallel paws propping triangular face
 eschewing the playful tease of
your favorite toy
After many good days — of sunshine
  and wholeness
Days when I don't cry, there are just as many
When cuffed by grief, my heart is holden
by your memories
When you lived in my house, and walked in the
  park
With me by your side.
Why is it that this grief — ebbs and flows
without warning or expectation,
resurfaces —
Reminding me that you lived, and breathed
That your life brought me joy —
And the work of training you
and the hardship of losing you

~ are all but byproducts of grief
I still long for your companionship
And your unconditional love, a love that
Touched me, moved me — even when I was
    wrong
Your acceptance — your unconditional friendship
Turned a faucet of repentance; because of you
I learned how to change
You accepted me for who I was —
All my faults and short comings, I saw myself
    through your eyes
And slowly learned how to love
How to give beyond my own boundaries,
in spite of people and "conditions"

How is it you taught me so many things, Car?

Recollections of You
6/5/19

Can I just say that I love you? That I miss you and your wonderful cuteness? That I miss your bigness and your huge canine chest—the one that I used to hug and wrestle with? I miss feeding you and giving you treats and making you sit, then lay down, then putting a bone on your nose for you to toss in the air, and catch. I miss you sitting by the front door and looking for me, watching out the window for squirrels—and chasing the neighbor's cat. The one you seemingly hated, that always outran you. She taunted you, and you'd bark at her unmercifully from the bedroom window.

    I miss you and our rides in the car, giving you bananas and allowing you to drink my coffee.

    Okay, I didn't so much allow you—you did it anyway. I miss you more than I could have ever known. I miss the times in my office when, doing my devotion, you'd lay there listening to every whispered prayer and watch every tear that fell. You heard me cry out to Jesus and often nuzzled right next to me. Your presence was a source of comfort I dearly miss, and long for.

Each month that passes I look back and think of you. What I was doing last year during the same month? What we were doing, where we were, how *you* were. Details I remember still etched in my mind. I took pictures. How often do you get to see a 50lb black dog sitting shotgun— enjoying a ride with the window down?

Mostly, I'm sad. Really sad. I miss you so much my heart hurts. I miss you to the moon and then some. Girl—you were with me through my father's death, and the aftermath of grief, the hardship of family relationships, struggles with midlife, and balancing a family with teens. When problems came up, it was me, you, and the trail where we'd beat out 4 or 5 miles.

You loved me unconditionally. You always listened.

I loved you in such a way—only a dog owner and lover could understand. People who don't own dogs can't begin to comprehend the depth and richness of such a companionship. There really are no words for my loss. My heart breaks and heals. Then breaks again, over and over. I am saddened and surprised by how deep my grief— this bereavement—is; it's overwhelming at times. Yet, I know in my heart it's a process, and a cycle of life. Things will get better.

~*~

Humanity is enlarged when a heart learns to love deeply, and then let go. To accept loss, to brave a new life and the (different) world it leaves in its wake.

    In all my understanding of love and loss, grief's wake was never meant to drown me, but rather, it offered a ripple—the buoyancy I needed to push me onward, forward.

Full Circle
9/13/19

I drove by Amanda's yesterday,
By the field where I stopped to let you out
Blades of green grass bowed as the wind danced
        across
an open meadow
Near the dry gully
Where you often squatted

And I remembered

Your long snout
Perpetually licking the bottom of my
Coffee cup

How we'd drive together
Your insistence to ride shotgun,
Peering out the window
Daring any man to approach

I drove by and recalled
Your love for the chase —
Poor squirrel
Poor cat
Any cat
       — Finding their 'tootsies'
Your breath was a telling sign

I drove by an old neighborhood
And thought of you,
The rear-view mirror refining my direction
In a wistfully bittersweet way

It's time.

Welcome Home
Rio

The New Guy in Town
9/9/19

His hair — wispy, black and wavy,
Is soft to the touch
The way he looks at me
Melts my heart

Energetic to a fault,
He wants to go out
All the time
Confident, frisky,
Always forgiving,
Even when I forget to call
We simply meet later
      ~ no sulking look

He's tender-hearted,
Unlike you. You,
with your brash ways — take-charge attitude
Were quite daunting at times

And though I know you loved me
Tenderness from you
Was a rarity

There's a new guy in town
With coal-colored eyes
And wavy black hair
Who loves me now

He lives on our block
— and sleeps on my bed
And I'm okay with that.

Welcome to the family
    ~ Rio

Broken Partition

*No longer
The sound of piety,
 — invisible barrier keeping me
from you*

*No longer an
allusion: child
reaching up,
needing assurance*

*No longer excluded
 — spiritual caste
separating, preventing,
forestalling deep intimacy
Of truths we hold:
you,
me*

*Your Name — just the sound
draws me
close,
bundling my soul
Heaven's breath
on my face;
a kiss
Eternal warmth*

No longer keep I,
you,
distant — arm's length
apart;
I call you Abba

Dedicated to the most Holy and One True God: no longer just my Savior, Friend, Companion, Lover, Husband, Provider...

    You are my Abba. My Father.

My Dearest Carlie,

When you were young, I called you 'Carlie-boo.' The name seemed to fit your energy for life; you'd sneak up on cats and squirrels and the chase was on . . .

You were never the "perfect child"—your obedience fell somewhere in between love for a tr-e-a-t and the lust of the chase. Even still, I loved you, your enthusiasm—your joy for life.

The years ticked by dotted with episodes of "chocolate fiascoes"—you ate entire boxes of Russel Stover chocolates, a known canine poison, and threw the entire house into a frenzy. But for the gifted advice of a sage vet and an emetic of peroxide, you lived through each incident.

You were a real help to me. A support in difficult times; a nurturer—but only to me. Fiercely protective, you never backed down. I felt safe in your company, enjoyed every run, and every cup of joe I never finished.

I know I was not the best dog parent. I had no real training or experience. But we both "schooled" each other, in the art of discipline and friendship. You taught me how to connect with you; I learned your habits and ways, anticipating your needs even into old age.

It was only then, at the end, that I understood the meaning of longsuffering as I watched your once virile body slowly embrace the toll of the years, of a life well lived.

I chided myself for things I could've done differently when you lived under my care— would'ves, should'ves, could'ves—took liberty with my vulnerability, battering my mind during the initial days of your passing. Thankfully after counsel with other dog parents, and much prayer, I came to peace within myself, reconciling your death as a natural course of life. Though at first it didn't feel "natural" to me.

Your life brought peace to my grieving heart after my dad's passing. To not have you meant revisiting grief's pain again. Normalcy was a vague term which slipped in and out of my mind; I struggled to rebalance, to find homeostasis— to find purpose and meaning again.

I measured each holiday with the previous one: where you were, where I was, what we did. The simple days and simple ways we lived our lives between activity, work, fun, rest. What did I have *now* to compare with? What could I measure my life against in the absence of a blank canvass? A canvass once smattered with days of hide-n-seek, of closets and socks, playing catch with MilkBones, and slinking around to hunt for anything peppermint.

Every car ride, every familiar park area, reminded me of you, your life—our life, our togetherness of fourteen years. It was hard. Very hard. Working through grief requires compassion and understanding. The ebb and flow of memories and emotions are healed through the passage of time, in new experiences, and in letting go.

It's been a year now. One complete year. Three hundred-sixty-five days. I've witnessed the full circle of life in raising and caring for you from beginning to end. It was the most difficult loss I have yet to process—because you were the first— my first. The first real death I'd encountered where, as an adult, I had to square off again with Grief.

I didn't know or understand Grief. He was a stranger who took up residency within my soul and laid dormant, sowing seeds of abandonment, rejection, anger—a veritable garden decorated with self-doubt and hatred. Little did I know that Grief—the acceptance of, and its refusal—can affect not only one's mental health, but one's emotional health as well.

Research suggests if all 5 stages of grief aren't processed, a person's state of being - their mindset, may become "locked" in one particular stage.

For example, someone who's not been able to grieve completely could easily be stuck in the stage of "denial." They just can't believe, won't believe, that things turned out like they did . . . they deny their heart the right to feel, to embrace the pain of loss, they deny the idea that anything bad really happened. They may even superimpose that same type of denial in their daily lives or work. They don't talk about the pain, the hurt, or they pretend nothing really bad happened.

It's denial. They're stuck.

Just like I was.

Epilogue ~ Inside Looking Out

The only way I could deal with the intense sadness after Carlie died was to write. Writing allowed me to think, to grieve privately—if only on paper. It was a simple act of pouring myself on to a page without judgment or second guessing.

Throughout this time, I also re-read excerpts from books or articles I'd previously saved which dealt with death, sorrow, and grief. I needed to understand myself and my seemingly profound sadness—over what? A dog? The thought of grieving the loss of a pet might seem strange to non-pet owners, and prior to losing Carlie, I too may have scratched my head . . . maybe.

But, while mourning her passing, thoughts of mortality, dying, of life on the other side - surfaced easily; images and feelings came in layers: some days I was okay, not great, but okay. Other days were intense. Almost unbearable.

Depression loomed as grief's bridle led me down dark roads; scenic roads from a distant past with haunting memories stuffed down so far, Grief's claw snagged the corner edge. And once hooked, it pulled violently, forcing me to look at more than just the sorrow of my beloved pet. During this time, I learned about unprocessed grief, where, when a person has not fully walked through the steps, when grief isn't completely processed you become "stuck" between stages. Through this lens—this stuck stage, be it anger or denial—life is then lived and interpreted. That's how I would describe my own process with grief: stuck.

The truth is Carlie's death had nothing and yet everything to do with my "stuck-ness." It happened years before, during a time in my childhood where, bounding down the front porch steps to hop on my bike, I was greeted by a Pastor, our minister from the church we occasionally attended. His arrival sparked a conversation among my siblings and my father which ended with intense sadness and confusion.

What did he say? What words spring boarded my dance with Grief?

"Your mother has died . . ."

These words hung in the air as the setting sun tipped its hat through the curtains of our suburban Minneapolis home. It sent the mind of a 9-year-old girl to a place far away—she plugged her ears, unwilling to listen anymore. If she didn't hear anything, it didn't really happen.

As I grew up, I waltzed with Grief off and on for many years: Distant Partner, Associate, Enemy—never Friend. Grief became the lens of anger from which I interpreted life. Unbeknownst to the benefactor of my rage, sometimes my suppressed anger fueled an argument, and even though I knew what was happening, I truly couldn't help myself; it was the ebb and flow of my personality.

Through therapy, I became acquainted with terms such as "unmet needs, and unprocessed grief." I became familiar with and learned about the stages of grief, and identified with certain behaviors victims of trauma adopt as coping mechanisms. Bingo! I could've easily become the poster child for deflection, avoidance, and anger—to name a few.

As an adult, carrying around Grief's baggage prevented me from seeing the "glass half full." As a 9-year-old, my view of family dramatically reframed itself. Ever the pessimist, I saw the world through the lens of 'a temporary standby;' things would change. People would enter and exit my life without consequence. Nothing would last forever. I was angry and didn't realize or understand how to work through or 'get over it' as people would say. Back then, counseling/therapy was hardly a topic for dinner table discussion. Counseling was meant for addicts and alcoholics, not for children who undergo a traumatic event like losing a parent. *Or is it?*

So it was, in my third decade of life, when things started to unravel. Truth be told, they'd been unraveling for a while—just gone unchecked, or better said: unnoticed. During this time, certain movies evoked flashbacks, words or phrases dredged up images from the past like a trolling fisherman whose line snags every weed or underwater plant. I noticed irregular patterns of intense anger and anxiety which surprised me. Most often I considered myself to be somewhat calm. But these patterns of irregular emotional behavior, (beyond PMS or hormonal imbalance) prompted me to read, research and seek guidance.

I landed in counseling (some call it therapy,) and was strongly encouraged to examine hurtful memories attached to any lingering trauma, and then begin to release them. I was instructed to 'unpack' my emotional baggage. *What does that even mean?* I had no clue.

Later on, after asking God for help, I realized my anger was tied to unprocessed grief; truth be told, I'd been "stuck between stages" for a while.

Though there are different models to explain grief, the one which resonated most to me was the Kubler-Ross Model. The five stages of grief are often described as: *Shock & Denial* ("I can't believe this happened"); *Anger* (a way to restore control); *Bargaining* ("if only it were me"); *Depression* (overwhelming regrets, nothing to look forward to); and *Acceptance* (coming to terms with, reconciling oneself in a sense of calm or of expectation, not fighting against, no struggle). Research suggests some folks skip stages, or they don't feel the full impact of certain ones, perhaps even all five stages. However, that may not be true for everyone. They may find themselves stuck in limbo—past the shock and denial, living in Anger Mode. It would be nice to say after just a few therapy sessions, coupled with learning more about the stages of the grief, that I walked in wholeness. But honestly, it was only the beginning.

The truth is, the journey through Carlie's death brought to surface areas of latent grief; the unresolved issues I *hadn't* laid to rest.

In reading through my journey, you may have noted the reference to Christmas, or my feeling robbed, thus the connection between past and present grief. Dealing with the loss of my beloved companion Carlie also dredged up childhood memories of losing my mom, memories I hadn't given voice to, as in the poem *Christmas Without You,* where I write about the first Christmas after she died. I had no idea the hand of Grief and I would waltz to her grave—time and time again.

My childhood grief had been carefully compartmentalized, vaulted and sealed. It'd become a cauldron of unprocessed emotional magma waiting to be dumped, and Carlie's passing was the tipping point. To empty out, to process both present grief and past was to give myself both time and permission to heal through all the stages of bereavement.

It was all connected.

Dear Reader, I want you to know how important you are to me. You've purchased this book, or you're holding it in your hand as a gift, and maybe you're wondering how to work through the rawness of pain and loss.

In most sports there's a scoreboard to determine when things end, which is not the case when it comes to bereavement. Though not everyone grieves the same way, for same number of days, weeks, or months, during your period of grief and mourning - leave time and judgment at the door - let the clock run out

Rest assured, this journal is not meant to make you feel uncomfortable; but rather, it's a tool to show how grief moved in one person's mind and heart, about how it's okay to feel pain instead of 'pushing it down' or burying it. And to know there are people just like you, like me, who don't know- or didn't know, how to process pain, voice fears, or share their hurt.

So, I wrote about it. And I prayed about it; I sought counsel from others—those a little further down the road with more wisdom. I did what I could to ease the ache, but it was the tenderness of God which mended my broken heart.

He whispered encouragement through His Word and surrounded me with loving people time and again to offer a text, phone call, or card – right when I needed it most. And He will do the same for you!

As you waltz through the stages of Grief, remember that on the other side, there's a different partner, patiently waiting to cut in and take your hand, named Peace.

Resources for Grief and Bereavement

In researching this section, I was surprised to learn that neither the Humane Society nor the Animal Control Shelter (Marion County, Florida) have resources for grieving the loss of a pet.

To that end, and with permission, copies of *Paws to Remember* will be offered to these organizations with the hope that others will, after waltzing with Grief like me, find comfort on the other side of Rainbow Bridge.

While this isn't an exhaustive list, the tools I've sourced below are personal resources within my library dealing with aspects of grief, written by authors whose work left an impact not only upon my life, but the world at large.

These writers have personal acquaintance with death, loss, and recovery. With artistic resolve, each author writes their heart, sharing their truth as they walk through healing, to wholeness.

- *When Breath Becomes Air* – Paul Kalanithi
- *Blue Nights* – Joan Didion
- *The Year of Magical Thinking* – Joan Didion
- *Autobiography of a Face* – Lucy Grealy
- *Love and Trouble: A Midlife Reckoning* – Claire Dederer
- *Heating & Cooling*; The Visitation (pg. 77), Grief's Vacation (pg. 99) – Beth Ann Fennelly
- *Psalm 34, Holy Bible*
- *My Grandfather's Blessings* – Rachel Naomi Remen, MD
- *Small Victories: Spotting Improbable Moments of Grace*; This Dog's Life (pg. 137) – Anne Lamott

- SAMHSA's National Helpline: 1-800-662-HELP (4357)
- How Right Now – howrightnow.org
- Creagan, Edward T. "Grieving Process: Is Crying Required?" Mayo Clinic, Mayo Foundation for Medical Education and Research, 15 May 2020.
- "Bereavement Counseling." U.S. Department of Veterans Affairs, 9 May 2006.

CPSIA information can be obtained
at www.ICGtesting.com
Printed in the USA
LVHW050304070723
751807LV00006B/234